Social Media Marketing:

*The Ultimate Guide
to Learn Step-by-Step
the Best Social Media
Strategies to Boost
Your Business*

Gerry T. Warner

Table of Contents

What This Book Will Teach You

Are you curious to learn about Social Media Marketing but unsure where to start?

Have you always wanted to learn more about Social Media, but are intimidated by the technical jargon being used?

If these questions relate well with you, then this book is for you. In this book, you will find the basic essentials to learning about Social Media Marketing. This book introduces readers on how to best leverage Social Media in marketing your products and services, by guiding you on the in's and out's and the various processes and steps involved in it.

Who this Book is for

This book contains information on how to learn about Social Media Marketing from a beginner level.

Readers who can benefit the most from the book include:

- Digital Marketing professionals who want to leverage Social Media in marketing their organization's products and services

- Creative individuals who want to learn about Social Media Marketing and how it can help their promote their works and make money off it

- Readers who would like to know information about Social Media Marketing

How this Book is Organized

This book is organized into three parts. The parts are best read in chronological order. Once you become familiar with all the steps outlined in the book, you can go directly to the techniques which apply to your current situation the best.

The three parts of the book are:

Part One outlines the essential topics on Social Media Marketing. The section also talks about how important it is to learn these topics as a beginner in order to form a solid foundation in doing the right steps – from introductory concepts to making your first Social Media Marketing campaign.

Part Two is about the profit side of Social Media Marketing, and how it actually helps you earn money selling products and services. You'll learn how the process works and how to implement the steps discussed.

Part Three dives deep into detail the different Social Media platforms (e.g. Facebook, Twitter, LinkedIn) and how to best use each for Social Media Marketing.

After each chapter, you will be provided with lessons and exercises in order to leverage the information found on this book.

By reading and implementing the steps outlined on this book, you will be able to understand Social Media Marketing essentials in helping you achieve your online marketing goals.

Introduction:

Welcome and thank you for purchasing *Social Media Marketing: The Ultimate Guide to Learn Step-by-Step the Best Social Media Strategies to Boost Your Business.*

Just a decade ago, Facebook was starting to become popular and sites such as Instagram, LinkedIn, and Snapchat had yet to come into existence. In today's world, the internet is extremely vast and offers every user a place to find answers, valuable intel, awesome products, and discover new businesses.

In 2018, however, starting any kind of business, both brick and mortar and online, can be difficult when it comes to getting your name out there for potential customers to see and visit you. There is so much competition you have to weasel your way through to become well-known, which makes this one of the top reasons why new businesses fail to succeed. Brand awareness is vital to make a business prosperous.

Social media is one of the most profitable marketing methods and is very stress-free and easy to learn. There are many folks just like you that have yet to take advantage of the benefits offered by social media platforms when it comes to the growth and visibility of your business.

There are thousands of websites out there that teach newbies what internet marketing is and how to make more money with their social media business accounts efficiently. This makes it a daunting task to figure out what information is the most accurate and up to date, let alone finding sources that are easy to understand and implement yourself.

This is why I am so excited you are here! With the help of this book, you will discover how to use social media platforms and unique marketing strategies to grow your business and increase your potential profits! All I ask of you is that you are willing to learn and take action. The internet is truly incredible, which is why you must make use of its potential to build a strong foundation that will make your business last. Are you ready?

Chapter 1: The Power of Social Media Marketing

Chapter 1 – The Power of Social Media Marketing

Just a couple of decades ago, the internet was barely a thought in people's minds, and business owners were depending on newspaper ads, paper flyers, and word of mouth to attract customers to their business. The world has changed greatly since then.

In 2018, businesses and individuals alike have been using the power and adaptability of the World Wide Web for a decade. Many folks have taken the time to learn how to create their own websites and establish a connection between the customers and their business. However, for regular folks like you and me, building websites, learning code and how to use site builders is not our thing. While websites are the bomb, there are other easier and more effective ways to attract customers to your awesome and growing business: social media!

What are social media and social media marketing?

Unless you have been living under a rock or held captive in a basement, I don't think I have to tell you just how large the presence of social media is. It's known as the quickest growing trend in the history of the entire world. Within just the first decade of these platforms being available to the public, the internet gathered around a billion users. Now that's a lot of peeps! In ten years, a sixth of the planet's total population will have their own social media accounts.

Social media

This is a term which refers to sites that provide different social actions for users. For example, Facebook is a broad social networking website that allows users to post photos and videos, share updates, join events and many other activities. Twitter, on the other hand, is designed for folks to share short messages with other users.

Social media marketing

This is the process in which people and businesses alike gain traffic and attention from varieties of other internet users and even other websites. Social media and social media marketing, as you can imagine, go hand in hand.

Social media allows thousands of internet users to come across new content, news, stories, businesses, and products. Social media is extremely useful in helping the search engine optimization efforts which build the foundation for long-term success in both brick and mortar and online business fronts. With social media, people from around the globe can connect to worldwide businesses with just the click of a mouse. Not to mention, social media platforms are becoming just as influential and popular as search engines like Google, YouTube, and Yahoo.

Social media essentially has a closely-knit connection to everything in the land of search engines since it can cover all aspects of internet marketing.

How social media marketing came to be

It might be hard to believe, but the popularity of social media did not start with the birth of Facebook. The idea of social media began way back in the early 1970's with the first email that was sent out in 1971. The very first site that was developed for social interacting online was called Six Degrees, which debuted in 1997. Listed below is the timeline:

- **1997** — Six Degrees was the very first social platform that enabled people to create profiles and befriend other users

- **2001** — StumbleUpon was launched and gave a new innovative approach to interacting

- **2002** — Friendster was born - like Six Degrees but with more of a focus on the capability to share articles

- **2003** — LinkedIn and MySpace were created during this time, which was both inspired by music

- **2004** — Facebook was officially founded

- **2005** — YouTube was created as a platform to share videos

- **2006** — Twitter was presented as the top website to host unique SMS text forms

- **2007** — Tumblr made its first debut as a short-form blogging platform that also allowed users to share content with specific groups of people

- **2010** — Instagram was launched and was the first site to offer photo sharing

- **2011** — Google launched Google+
- Google also launched Snapchat, the first ever photo and video experience

- **2012** — Pinterest was born and was coined as a 'social scrapbooking' website

- **2012** — Vine was also launched and allowed users to created 6-second videos with the ability to loop

- **2015** — Periscope was the first app created with live streaming capabilities

Why understanding history is vital to social media success

If you are anything like me, history class was my least favorite class growing up. I was much more intrigued with what is happening in the present than how America won wars to get to where we are today. Terrible of me? Yeah, probably. But when it comes to social media marketing, there is a good reason why beginners should take the opportunity to grasp the history of the internet.

Not only will you visualize the rapid development and advancements of each platform over the years, but you will also see firsthand the unique qualities that each one offers users. By seeing the pitfalls and outdated applications for what they are, you are not wasting time on platforms that are dying out and are ready to be educated in what is to come, which is essential in keeping the pace with other expert marketers.

Social media trends are constantly changing, which is why you should always be aware of the creation of new content, what your target audiences want and need, and the varying ways you can make a living from the creation of an online business.

Uses of social media marketing

It's obvious that social media lights up almost every corner of the world and continues to expand, but how exactly does it affect the brand, engagement, and revenue of companies both on and offline?

Social media has made it possible to literally manipulate the way potential customers see a brand, product, and business. This is why it can be overwhelmingly frustrating to see other people making it big in the social media marketing realm while you are still struggling. (No worries, you have a lot to learn, and we will get you all caught up!)

There are many uses of social media when it comes to marketing, but in 2018, there are a few specific uses that are trending and causing a riot on the internet.

The main uses for social media marketing

To collaborate on passions and interests

Being able to use social media today is not a heroic act, but people try to make it look like one. To make the best out of social media, one needs to establish the passions and interests that their target audience has. This can take some time to figure out, but it will happen over time.

For instance, if you are a portrait photographer, you really should be putting your best work on at least one social media platform so you can promote your work and gain more customers.

When you can depict your interest properly to others, you are a step ahead already. When you market yourself as a product to the world, you have greater chances of making things work. Plus, the use of hashtags and keywords will certainly help.

To stay in touch

Thanks to the internet, even the average Joe can reach out to their audience even if they're thousands of miles away. This creates a communicative bridge between you, your audience, and future consumers. Dig deep into what your audience wants and needs, as well as trends, to hit your target.

Platform for the proper tools

You can't build a house without a hammer and some nails, right? The same goes for marketing on social media. Using and knowing the right tools is what separates successful online entrepreneurs from the perpetual newbies. You must stay in touch with your general audience to have ever-lasting prosperity.

Social media platforms have an array of tools built in that allow folks to analyze their numbers and change things up to gain more traction.

Brings people together

If you desire to become more of a public figure than a household name, then knowing how to use social media is a must. Your audience wants to know what you are doing, how you are doing it and why. Answer these questions, and you will have curious individuals addicted to you and coming back for more.

An audience is a vital component of building a following on social media for your business. Your customers are the glue that holds your business together! Internet platforms are easy-to-use ways that bring a variety of people together.

Brand recognition

Brand recognition is essential to building a business and can be done simply with the help of social media marketing. It's all about working to maintain the image of your brand:

- Indulge your audience with valuable conversations in your point of view
- Know what is trending about your brand
- Allow people the door to keep up with your brand and the content

Capture the attention of existing and new customers

Online marketing gives one the tools to reach brand new customers on a daily basis, which is why the ability to share and like videos, statuses, photos, and more with ease is vital.

Every single comment, video, article, and image is an opportunity for someone to react and engage with you and your brand, with the hope to eventually converse. While not every online action is an immediate conversion, you will still reach out to a broader audience.

Influence

Once you increase your reach, you now have the power to greatly influence others with your brand. This is vital to your success and should not be overlooked. The more you utilize social media, the more power you have to influence your main audience.

Direct traffic to website

I like to picture and explain to beginners that social media accounts are small doorways that lead people to your home, a.k.a. your brand's website. Social media is an amazing way to generate traffic and leads. You can promote new images, inspiring or educational videos, and post new blog posts to get folks to click on your link, head to your site, and potentially buy a product of yours.

To get ahead of the competition

Social media gives even new business owners an advantage and enough headspace to breathe as they figure out the ins and outs of getting ahead in a competitive industry.

Rise of authority

As you level up in the world of online marketing, you will discover how important it is to establish a sense of authority with your audience. This essentially means that no matter what topic your brand is centered around, if you are an authoritarian, you become the go-to place that when people seek answers and assistance.

Therefore, it's crucial to interact with your audience and develop an understanding of what they are struggling with and desire. By relating to your audience, you are focused on their minds which will eventually draw them to you.

Exposure

Exposure is key if you wish to continuously attract existing and potential consumers back to your website over and over again. While this can become monotonous, trust me, it pays off! Exposure is something you don't want to miss out on, especially if you are a growing business.

Grabbing existing customers

Loyal customers are the backbone of your online business, and social media is a superb way to get in touch with them, share new content and products that leave them wanting more from you. Keep up your efforts that brought them to you in the first place, make that originality a key part of your overall brand, and you will have old and new customers eating right out of the palm of your hand!

This might all sound pretty daunting to you, but I assure you that throughout this book you will learn methods that will allow you to absorb the knowledge required for you to take the internet and your brand by storm via social media platforms. Just keep reading!

The benefits of understanding social media marketing

Social media marketing was once considered a temporary fad that many entrepreneurs overlooked. Well, it's certainly a trend that has yet to step out of the spotlight.

Since social media was born and grew so rapidly, it received a reputation as a passing interest, but statistics over the last few years prove that theory wrong. In 2014, 92% of marketers said that marketing on social media was vital for the health of their business, with 80% saying that this increased effort brought much more traffic to their websites, according to Hubspot. So, if this doesn't speak for itself, I don't know what does!

Benefits of marketing your brand or business on social media

- Increased recognition of your brand

- Increase in customer loyalty
- Better opportunities for conversions
- High conversion rates
- Increased authority
- Better inbound/direct traffic to website(s)
- Lowered marketing costs
- Increased rank in popular search engines
- Ability to give customers a richer experience
- Better consumer insights

There have been a few studies that have proven that the usage of social media has a 100 percent higher rate than any outbound marketing technique and a much higher number of followers. This results in improved trust and credibility for your brand. You have to view social media as pure proof of the value you can offer to other people.

The longer you wait to start the creation of social media platforms that are associated with your brand and business, the more you lose out on. When done properly, social media marketing leads you to future customers and gains you more traffic and conversions, which is what all online entrepreneurs want. Keep reading to learn how to get started!

Chapter summary

- The idea of social media has been around for many decades

- Popular social media platforms may have been born a decade ago, but are continuing to grow in popularity

- The various uses of social media marketing are skills which are essential to the success and growth of businesses and brands
- These platforms make it easier for both new and experienced online entrepreneurs to get their name out there and attract consumers
- The benefits of using social media marketing tactics far outweigh the negativities of not utilizing them

Quickstart action step

Before you flip that page and continue to the next chapter, I urge you to read the following sources that dive deeper into the basics of social media marketing and what it can do to help grow your brand.

- The Top 30 Social Media Marketing Articles You Need to Read
  https://blog.wishpond.com/po

st/115675436687/social-media-marketing

- Why Social Media Marketing is Important for Any Business https://www.contentfac.com/9-reasons-social-media-marketing-should-top-your-to-do-list/
- Social Media and Content Marketing Trends That Will Shape 2018 https://www.forbes.com/sites/forbesagencycouncil/2018/01/11/social-media-and-content-marketing-trends-that-will-shape-2018/#47bb401d33d7
- The Top 10 2017 Social Media and Content Marketing Articles http://www.convinceandconvert.com/baer-facts/our-top-10-2017-social-media-and-content-marketing-articles/

Chapter 2: Why Social Media Marketing *Works*

Chapter 2: Why Social Media Marketing Works

When it boils down to utilizing social media platforms to transform your business and allow ample room to grow, it requires businesses to have a good strategy coupled with effort and dedication. Social media is the largest portion of the internet and rightfully so!

With 2 billion people who have an active Facebook account alone, it is safe to say that there is extreme power to be had behind this whole marketing business. If you need further proof of what social media can do for your business or personal brand, then this chapter is for you! Let's dive into why social media marketing has a cool way of making things happen and see the hidden benefits that this type of marketing has over other forms.

First, let me mention that there are many businesses and individuals that merely venture into the vast world of social media who expect to see substantial returns on their investments. Their hope is that a load of new consumers will come in and the generation of revenue will be ginormous. This is rarely the case. It takes dedicated time to build the momentum you need for your social media to reach the attention of potential customers, which makes the following benefits not as obvious at first glance.

Competitive advantage

If you are feeling a bit skeptical, I want you to stop that negative thinking for one moment; you are not the only one struggling to make social media work for you! There are many competitors in your industry that are not doing a very swell job at media either. Instead of staying in the newbie crowd, use the time you have now to become a seasoned expert in social media marketing so that you can stand above the crowd!

On the other hand, if you fail to embrace social media, you are leaving a gaping hole for one of your competitors to step in and take your thunder. Act now!

Brand recognition

One of the best ways to utilize social media is as a tool to build your brand. You get to choose how you wish to position your company with social media and what you want your customers to know. With effort and consistently awesome content, you can create a bright reputation where customers will know what you believe in, your core values, and your advantages over other similar businesses.

Community

Social media is also an amazing tool for cultivating a community around your brand. When you gain followers, they become part of your community, which allows you to gain access to a variety of people worldwide. This means you can figure out what they need and want, problems they are facing, etc. and center your business around helping people live a better life.

Repeated exposure

Did you know that it takes six to ten exposures to the same product before consumers click that 'buy' button? Social media allows companies to expose their products and services time and time again within their network. Reminding your followers consistently will help to shorten your sales cycle over time.

Build authority

There are thousands of websites online that are known as authority sites. What websites do you head to when you have specific questions about something you own or a product you want to buy? In the online world, you want to work hard to become an authority that folks trust and turn to for valuable information and advice.

Authority is especially important for speakers, consultants, authors, coaches, and any other businesses that are service-based. Social media is a powerful tool in helping regular folks like you and me establish authority, even in broad fields.

Influence

As you increase your following, you will find that a snowball effect happens that automatically attracts new consumers and many more exciting opportunities. Imagine seeing a crowd hovered over something intriguing; you can't help but want to know what all the fuss is about. The larger your audience, the more potential buyers will be attracted to your business and what you have to offer.

Traffic to website

Social media is the number one generator of website traffic; from videos, images, blog posts, and a variety of other content, you provide your audience with a reason to click the URL to your website and take a look around.

When visitors step upon the threshold of your website, this is when the magic can begin! You can inspire them to take action, sign up for an email list, buy a product, invite them to schedule a call with you, etc. Ensure that visitors are greeted with a clear and concise call to action when stumbling upon your website so that they are then converted to paying consumers.

Get ahead of the curve

Whether you want to believe it or not,

your competition, as well as prospective clients and consumers are checking to see how engaged you are with social media. In today's world, it tends to look odd when one goes to find or investigate a potential product, service, and/or business and they are unable to locate you on any social media platform.

Worse yet is a client stumbling upon a Facebook business page that you have failed to update in months or years. Social media is not going anywhere; even if it's not your top priority at this time, just keep in mind that potential consumers *will* take notice.

Share your mind

If you are wondering if anyone is even paying attention to your social media presence, I can guarantee they are much more than you even realize. When you are patient and consistent in your social media presence, you will begin to grasp what is happening behind all the anonymity of the World Wide Web. You will eventually hear from those that have loved your content for ages! What a great feeling, right?

Achieve bigger wins

There are thousands of businesses, both big and small that are all trying to justify their investment of money and time into marketing on social media. There is a huge aspect that is often overlooked, which is more substantial wins!

For instance, say someone on LinkedIn connects with you and wants you to get involved with them via contract, this would be qualified as a "big win." When actively on social media, you are creating a presence for yourself that can be seen worldwide.

Keeps your company honest

The internet, while amazing in many aspects, is also full of rumors and creatively wild fibs, and social media can be a platform that gives these sorts of folks a voice as well. Comments, tagging, ratings, and content allow your consumers to take a peek at your online business and speak their thoughts. This is more positive than negative for brands, even though it does sound intimidating. Negative comments even have the power to make your business shine when you are active and use these as opportunities for damage control.

Helps you remain relevant

Social media is so much more than simply connecting with friends and long-lost relatives. The majority of users utilize social media platforms to network and promote themselves, as well as to become more knowledgeable about their industries. Leaders add articles and stories that are relevant to their companies and industries. This builds authority, and seeing the comments and posts from their competition gives them the advantage to stay relevant to what customers want and need, which keeps them coming back for more.

Chapter 3: How to Increase Sales with Social Media Marketing

SOCIAL MEDIA

Chapter 3: How to Increase Sales with Social Media Marketing

As you can imagine, social media is one of the most essential marketing tools in today's era; how is one to utilize these powerful websites to build their brand and gain legit, substantial profit? This chapter will cover ways to increase sales through a variety of social media platforms.

Tell your brand's story

Social media is great at allowing people to create, propagate, and amplify their stories to consumers and followers. This enables people to connect with your brand on a deeper, emotional level. It gives people visual points and allows you to create a target market. When done correctly, social media will allow you to continuously build your story and gain exposure steadily.

Utilize brand ambassadors

Influence is *everything* in the world of social media marketing, so leverage the power of folks that are already highly known and influencing the internet. When you collaborate with these people, you are representing your company within their circles as well, which is a great way to gain new consumers and learn more about your target market.

Use a cross-platform strategy

It's is very crucial to have some sort of presence on a variety of social media platforms; while it can be daunting to find the time to keep track of them all, when you have a cross-platform strategy in place it will graciously make up for the lack of total dedication. Just be sure to prioritize each platform you make an account on since it will further optimize your peak efficacy.

Only use content that performs the best

You need to become knowledgeable about what your loyal fans love and don't like so much. When you have a crystal-clear idea of the content that your followers enjoy, you can constantly repeat that performance and gain substantial traction and sales.

- Posts that have a high performance = better chance of conversion
- Post with poor performance = lower conversions and loss of fans

Take advantage of user-generated content

User-generated content has been proven to perform greater than shots of regular products. What does this mean? That you should utilize it in the following ways:

-   *As a gallery on-site:* Give your consumers a bit of love by showcasing their content on platforms like Instagram. This encourages customers and fans to share their journeys with your company, and you get to reap all those awesome benefits of further exposure!

- *In addition to images:* Use earned content to showcase how your consumers can make what you sell their very own. Content from users provide better context and help potential buyers to see themselves using your products and services.

Benefits of social media

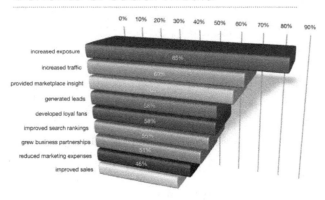

Quality over quantity, <u>always</u>

This is an obvious one, but there are plenty of mediocre companies with bogus websites that post crap content that helps no one, especially their conversions. Consistency is the biggest key to keeping up with an active online presence, but you should never post content that can be detrimental to your company standards. Post only high-quality images and articles!

Engage with your community

When you create a presence on social media, you are essentially building a community to grow over time. In order to gain visibility and give your company a boost, you need to make engaging with existing and potential followers a priority. This will not only help you gain followers but retain them, which means better conversions for your website!

Place a link in your bio(s)

When you add a link that allows visitors to directly go to your site, this aids in much better sales! The proof is pretty much in the pudding, just saying! If you have a new product or service, place that link in your bios! You want those links to gain the attention of a variety of people to gain exposure.

Dedicate a place for customer support

Some social media, like Snapchat and Instagram, are go-to tools for brand building while other platforms such as Facebook and Twitter are conduits for information. You have better opportunities to directly connect and communicate with your consumers on information based social media. It's much simpler to gather feedback and relay the details of orders.

Use Instagram ads

- Use correct visuals that will aid in the performance of content and resonate with Instagram audiences.

- Pick the right format for the message you wish to convey to your following and potential customers. Ensure that you add a clear and concise call to action as well.

- Wisely target your audience. Are you picking the correct demographic, interests, and location?

- I recommend using *this tool* (https://blog.dashhudson.com/easy-instagram-sponsored-ads-paid-social-advertising-strategy/) to ensure that you can create extremely effective Instagram ads that will catch the eyes of your followers and potential consumers of your business.

Capitalize on trends in content

Trends, fads, and hype ignite the desire to purchase, which makes researching trends an essential part of creating ads, products, and service that appeal to people. Be careful when diving into in-the-moment fads since they may only be relevant for a very short period of time. Ensure you tickle the fancy of people that make them click happy to buy from you. It's all about the sound of the sale!

Build a gifting program

If you can manage it, send out products to micro influencers and content creators. This will help you to:

- Spread your name
- Increase desirability of what your company has to offer
- Produce a large amount of content for you to repurpose and utilize
- Help grow your community

All of the above tips will help you to further translate your social media platform dedication to abundant sales and a great customer following. Ensure you have a great profile that attracts people as well, which further lines your wallet.

Only do what your current company budget allows for. Otherwise, you will fail to truly align with your business and its objectives. Not all companies have the proper funds to dedicate to giving

away free products. This can be
frustrating, but this is where
persistence, consistency, and patience
come into play when building your
business!

Chapter 4:
Top Social Media
Platforms - and
the Best Ways to
Use Them

Chapter 4: Top Social Media Platforms - and the Best Ways to Use Them

Social media platforms are an essential tool to build company brands, further our audience reach, and grow businesses for the better! However, there are still many businesses that are failing to take action to capture the power of social media.

Many people feel that they don't have the money for ad investment. Others are not yet convinced that a presence on social media is great for their business or a great use of resources and time.

That is why as a beginner, you need to be aware of what social media platforms are the most popular and how to utilize them to their fullest potential to raise conversions, gain followers, and showcase your brand. This chapter will cover the most popular social media websites and how anyone can use them without spending a bunch of time or money to capitalize on them!

Twitter

Twitter is just about for *everyone* and is the only <u>free</u> platform that helps to drive traffic to your websites in as few as three to four days. The best thing about Twitter is that there is no reason to constantly be on it all the time and there are easy ways to make it appear like you are. There are many tools out there such as *Hootsuite* that allows you to create a bunch of tweets all at once, with you being the wizard that picks the times for them to post!

Once tweets are scheduled, you can hop onto the platform and respond to comments and inquiries. You only have to be active for about 10 minutes at a time, but you can make it look like you are on there a heck of a lot more.

Become an advocate of mastering hashtags as well, but be sure to not go overboard with them. Alternate between hashtags that are relevant to your business and posts.

Facebook

Facebook is another platform that just about everyone can easily use and a site that most of the world has an account for. Facebook is an awesome tool if you have the time and energy to put into it.

I recommend posting a chunk of content every time you post on Facebook. "Chunks" include three to five pieces of content:

1. Blog
2. Video
3. Image
4. Link
5. Content written by you
6. Content written by someone else (consumers, ghostwriter, etc.)
7. Content from another blog in your industry
8. Article or magazine links

When it comes to Facebook ads, they are much better to use than Twitter ads. For just 5 dollars you can boost a post of your business in front of an additional 2000-3000 Facebook users, which is pretty darn substantial!

LinkedIn

LinkedIn is a great platform to use if you are looking for clientele and consumers that are more professional. You can share blog posts, communicate effectively, and add users in high-ranked places, such as CEO's, business owners, etc.

You will get the most out of LinkedIn if you actively join groups (https://www.forbes.com/sites/williama rruda/2015/09/30/the-best-way-to-get-started-with-linkedin-

[groups/#7526c23c7e20)](groups/#7526c23c7e20) and share targeting information that will attract others to the group and connect with you.

Instagram

Instagram is an easy-to-use a social media platform that is not as time-consuming as some other websites. If you consistently post at least once per day and utilize hashtags wisely, you can gain a substantial number of followers that will turn into potential customers that will raise your overall conversions.

The best part about Instagram is how visual the platform is; blog photos are more appealing and make people want to click on your links. All you have to do is add tiny snippets of information about what posts, products, or services are about to attract people to visit your website. You can now post videos, as well as live feeds to Instagram as well.

Pinterest

Pinterest is another platform that is similar to Instagram and is renowned for its ability to be highly visual. Pinterest is the perfect platform for those that sell products within their companies. It also works great for those that have tips they want to provide their loyal fans, especially tips related to organizing, decorating, and home improvement.

The downside of Pinterest is that you will need to dedicate a good chunk of time on it since it's one of those platforms you will have to be on consistently to do great on. It's recommended to post to Pinterest at least twice per day, so you are more likely to reach people. It takes some time to like boards, follow people and influencers, and connect with fans, consumers, and authorities of your brand. Pinterest may take more hard work, but when you put that additional time and effort in, your business is sure to gain tons of value from it!

Find what works for you and <u>stick with it!</u>

No matter what industry you and/or your company is in, nothing will ever happen overnight. When you are a beginner creating your business online, you will have to be willing to experiment with social media platforms, applications, online tools, etc. to find the best practices and what increases your sales the most.

When you stick consistently with your efforts, you will become a more seasoned online entrepreneur! Be prepared to learn as you grow. Trust me, there are tons of business owners online that are still learning the tides of social media marketing themselves. As the internet changes, be prepared to have to get on the learning curve to keep up.

Chapter 5: Facebook

Chapter 5: Facebook

Before we dive into the amazing world of Facebook, let me put its power into perspective for you; the world population is just over 7.5 billion, and one out of every four people on the entire planet has a Facebook account.

As you can imagine, Facebook is continuously taking over the world, with over 62% of North America alone using the platform daily. The percentages of other countries are quite staggering as well, and the diagram below is representative of 2016, which leaves two whole years to consider:

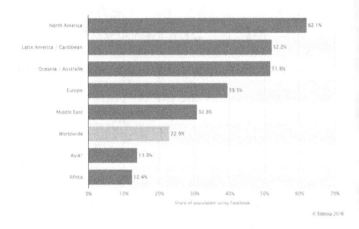

Facebook, in many ways, is its own little country all by itself. The population on Facebook is bigger than any other country's population in the world, and you can even argue that it's much more connected. And guess what? This is just Facebook. We aren't even talking about other social media platforms yet!

What is Facebook?

Even people who don't have their own account know the basics of what Facebook is about, it's a social networking website that is easy to use to connect with family, friends, co-workers, classmates, your fifth cousin twice removed, your neighbor's dog, and many others.

Facebook was originally created with college students in mind in 2004 by the infamous Mark Zuckerberg while he himself was enrolled at Harvard University. Just two years later, anyone over 13 years of age that had an email address could sign up for a Facebook account.

Why should you use Facebook?

So, why do more than a billion people like using the Facebook interface? There are tons of other alternatives when it comes to connecting online, such as instant messaging and email. Facebook is unique in the capability it gives users to share and connect with others.

Facebook is now a standard aspect of being engaged in the online world, much like having an email address. Since Facebook is so renowned, thousands of other websites have found ways to integrate Facebook into their interfaces as well. This means that with just a single Facebook account, you can sign into a bunch of services across the World Wide Web.

Ways to use Facebook

- View updates and posts from Facebook friends
- Share videos and photos
- Share information via your profile page
- Invite friends to join Facebook groups and events
- Chat with friends and other Facebook users
- Play games and utilize applications
- Connect with businesses and celebrities
- Use social plug-ins
- Connect Facebook account with other websites for ease of access

How sharing on Facebook works

Facebook's platform easily allows you to

send messages and post updates to keep in touch and update family and friends. There are many different kinds of content you can share on Facebook, from photos, videos, reposts, and links, etc.

Sharing things on Facebook is slightly different from other websites, however.

Unlike the privacy of instant messaging and email, things shared on Facebook are much more public and can be seen by other people, even people who are not your Facebook friends.

This is where privacy tools and settings come into play to limit who can see what is on your profile until you accept their friend requests.

Facebook is designed to be an open interface to enhance the overall social experience, which makes it vastly divergent compared to similar social media sites and other communication tools.

Benefits of using Facebook as part of a social media marketing strategy

1. Low cost: You don't have to have any money upfront to create a personal or a business Facebook account

2. Access to millions of target audiences

3. Can be used to share any information and value related to your brand

4. Very interactive interface

5. Allows businesses to directly communicate with existing and potential customers

6. Provides more than adequate customer support

7. Traffic to websites can be easily scaled higher

8. Easy to raise awareness of your brand through likes and sharing

How to market with Facebook

business pages

Facebook pages are essentially the easiest method to beginning your journey in Facebook marketing. They are free, simple to build, and very flexible. There are many companies on Facebook that fail to use their business pages to their full potential. Use these guidelines to avoid common mistakes:

Profile and cover photos

1. Your profile photo should ideally be your logo
2. Use your cover photo to be more creative
    1. Photos of employees
    2. Fancy artwork
    3. Contact information

4. Pick an image that further enhances your page and attracts visitor's eyes

'About' section

Placed below your company logo, this is your shot at informing people who visit your page what your business is all about:

1. What does your company do?
2. Why are you different from the competition?
3. What kind of other interesting details can make you stand out?

Write this portion specifically for visitors. You can use this same content on your website and/or blog as well.

Don't forget to fill in the 'Basic Info' section in its entirety:

1. Be informal and friendly
2. Use a casual tone

Tabs

Tabs are the squares that are placed at the right of the 'About' section. Facebook allows up to 10 tabs, which to admins is known as the 'Favorites' section.

What priorities do you have for your visitors?

1. Do you have a physical store? Make sure you have a 'location' tab

2. Do you host webinars? Make sure to include an 'events' tab

Post useful and valuable content on your wall

The content you posted on your Facebook page ends up in the newsfeed of followers. You want to ensure you are posting engaging, valuable content that will attract more likes and reactions, as well as a growing following.

Post content to your fans that they will get the most use out of, such as:

3. Links to online tools
4. Announcements of new products

5. Codes for coupons to save money on your products or services
6. Links to blog posts
7. Links to any articles that are related to your company's industry

Ask questions

Fans enjoy getting involved with your business via Facebook, and this is a superb opportunity to inspire their long-term loyalty to you. When you ask your followers questions, this gives them a chance to get involved but on their terms:

1. Ask open-ended questions so that you receive the best and unique responses

2.   Ask people's opinions to show that you care about what they want and need

The more engagement you can get on each post, the better! You want your content to reach the very top of the Facebook news feed.

Don't be spammy

No one likes a spammer, especially companies that do so in an attempt to attract new consumers. Spamming is probably the fastest way to lose people. Before you send out any updates, ask yourself if it can add value to a conversation. If not, delete and start over.

If you are only sending out promotional content without any value, you are making it difficult to keep fans.

Study your results

Facebook is one of the many social media platforms that offer an amazing page to review your analytics. This is something you should learn to read and keep a close eye on. If you see a downward surge of fans, look what you have posted recently. If you see a positive upswing of fans, then repeat this type of content.

8 easy steps to creating a great Facebook business page

Step 1: Sign up

1. Head to facebook.com/business and click on 'Create a Page.'
2. Select your type of business
   1. Does business fall into more than one category? Pick the one that customers will likely think about as your business

3. Fill in details and sub-categories
4. Click 'Get Started.'

Step 2: Add images

5. Upload a profile picture and a cover photo. Ensure they align well with your brand, for these aid in a customer's overall first impression.

Step 3: Explore

6. Congrats! Your page is live!
7. Click through the prompts, so you learn where everything is located

Step 4: Write a business description

8. Keep this short, sweet, and to the point, 155 characters max

9. Use this opportunity to tell people about your business

Step 5: Create a username

10. Your username is also referred to as your vanity URL, which is how people find you via Facebook

11. Should be easy to type and recall
12. Click 'Create a Username for Your Page' to setup

Step 6: Complete the about section

13. Fill out all your business details as soon as you can since this is the first area a customer is likely to visit

14. Edit your story

15. Give a detailed description of what your business offers and what makes you stand out

16. Specify location

Step 7: Make your first post

17. Before you begin adding people to like your page, create some engaging and valuable content first

    1. Article/blog post
    2. Event
    3. Product offer

Step 8: Begin engaging

18. Now that you have some content on your Facebook

page and possibly some eager followers, engage with other pages and users.

Optimize your page by

19. Creating a call to action on your page or through messaging
20. Add pinned posts
21. Get the most bang for your buck with your tabs
22. Like other pages in your industry
23. Review settings to ensure proper setup
24. Learn from your insights page
25. Link your page to other web pages – your website or blog

26. <u>Get verified</u>

Proof of the power of Facebook

Less than a year ago, my business wanted to revamp our workspace and go someplace where we could be more creative without limitations. We wanted a giant dry-erase board but had no idea how to make that idea come to life. A quick Google search led us to the Facebook page of <u>IdeaPaint</u>, which is a B2B business that specializes in converting walls and other parts of your space into dry-erase surfaces to write on.

One of the biggest keys to building customer loyalty long-term is to provide your consumers with a great first experience with what you are selling. IdeaPaint goes above and beyond, providing visitors with videos sprinkled on their Facebook homepage, detailed tutorials to teach users how to do DIY projects, and a big ole tab that welcomes you into the hot spots to their other social sites.

Go and have a look at IdeaPaint's

Facebook page and website. They do a superb job in using several social aspects in their Facebook videos and photos. Paired with the traditional 'Like' button is the 'Send' button, which is a sneaky little call to action that encourages visitors to send their links to their friends.

IdeaPaint also creatively used networked blogs to help automate their blog posts to their own tab which is dedicated to posts on their Facebook page. This allows them to further enhance their news feed and capture the eye of potential customers. Plus, a giant dry-erase board is a great idea!

Chapter summary

1. Facebook is one of the most influential and easy-to-use social media platforms you can utilize to grow your business and collect loyal fans

2. Ensure you are posting content that your followers will find entertaining and valuable to read. Include a call to action!

3. There are a great number of ways to utilize Facebook. Experiment with them to find what works the best for your business and personal pages

4. Facebook is a platform that over a billion people are on. Leverage the power of people by creating a business around a prominent desire or need to attract more followers

5. Creating a Facebook business page and sticking with it is easy! Make it a habit to review your analytics page to polish up your content

Quickstart action step

Before you dive into the next chapter that discusses the social platform Twitter, I recommend you to take a few minutes and explore the Facebook business page setup process. Through the 8 easy-to-understand steps, you can have your page up and running in a matter of 10 minutes!

Don't put it off, start today! You cannot grow customer engagement if you fail to even begin the process of creating a page! If you get stumped at all, <u>here is a website</u> (<u>https://blog.hootsuite.com/steps-to-create-a-facebook-business-page/</u>) that can help you out with the above steps and more!

Chapter 6:
Twitter

Chapter 6: Twitter

Twitter is a social media platform that was created in 2006 designed for users to communicate in short messages known as tweets. 'Tweeting' is the action of sending short messages to any one of your followers. The idea is to tweet unique messages that capture the eyes of your audience because they're captivating and interesting. You could consider Twitter to be today's version of microblogging.

Many people utilize the Twitter platform to simply come across intriguing people and online companies and follow their Twitter profiles to stay up to date on current events.

Why Twitter is so popular

The thing that appeals to many Twitter users is how efficient and friendly the interface is. You can easily track hundreds of other users and read their content with a single glance. This is obviously ideal for a society that does not have high levels of patience.

Twitter allows users to post messages with purpose since the messages are restricted to a maximum of 280 characters or less. This helps to promote more focused language, which makes tweets simple to read and challenging to write. But thanks to the size restriction, Twitter is still a very popularized social tool, with over 970 million people using the interface.

How Twitter Functions

Twitter, like Facebook, is simple to use, even for beginners. You sign up for a free account and create a Twitter name. You can send out messages on a daily basis, even hourly or every minute if you desire. All you have to do is type your update in the 'What's happening' box and click the 'tweet' button. Easy peasy!

To fill up your Twitter feed with interesting content, you can follow a variety of users, from CEOs of companies, celebrities, and your run-of-the-mill folks like you and me. Just 'follow' them and subscribe to their tweet microblogs for their updates to fill up your feed. If there is a tweeter that becomes boring or is posting content you don't want to see or read, all you have to do is 'unfollow' them.

Why people tweet

People sign up and utilize the Twitter platform for various reasons, many of which are pretty useless, such as self-promotion, attention, and vanity, etc.

But there are plenty of other tweeters

that are using Twitter in a much more acceptable manner, they use it as a streamlined platform to provide followers with quick updates. Twitter has given people the ability to empower those that are just beginning their entrepreneurial journeys, allowing them to describe and share their experiences.

Yes, as you can imagine, there is a ton of nonsense and invaluable content on Twitter, yet, it can be a great base to grow your audience and provide news and valuable content to followers who are familiar with your business.

Twitter as a marketing tool

Between all the memes, funny quotes, and boring updates, you will find that

Twitter is home to many business-minded individuals who use Twitter as a recruiting technique that works wonders.

Internet-savvy users are sick and tired of advertisements on television. Folks today like more efficient and less intrusive advertising that can be turned on and off. Twitter is precisely that, giving business owners a unique step above the rest with good advertising results.

Twitter is a melting pot

If you view Twitter as a melting pot of texting, blogging, messaging, and communicating, you are completely right. It allows regular users and business owners to interact in brief context with a very broad audience. If you are a creative writer, Twitter is a great platform to showcase a creative content that people will find valuable to explore.

Ways to use Twitter as a business marketing tool

With more than 53 million active tweeters in the United States alone, Twitter can be a very powerful tool for marketing your business when used correctly. But how can beginners even leverage the power of limited characters to drive traffic to their website and business? Here's how:

Optimize bio

Ensure that your business's identity and voice is well branded. Create a bio that informs visitors who you are and include company links to landing pages and/or websites. The key is to use a consistent tone, so people understand clearly who you are and what your business does.

Who are the influencers in your target area?

Twitter is an optimum searching tool when it comes to finding and following customers, influencers, and other like-minded prospects. All you simply do is search keywords from your industry then you locate and interact with these people on a regular basis.

I recommend creating a list of at least 100 people that are influential in your online space such as bloggers, writers, clients, leaders, and journalists, etc. Add them to private lists and motivate yourself to engage with them often. Since Twitter is designed to be both casual and helpful, you can easily build relationships and will receive unique opportunities to work or collaborate with these famous individuals.

Get co-workers involved

The very first people you should have on your side when building up your brand is everyone on your internal team. Ensure that your colleagues are following you and each other on Twitter and are tweeting, retweeting, and engaging as well.

Tweet consistently

When you regularly tweet, this informs new and existing followers that you have an active profile. If you tweet just a couple times per week, you aren't keeping up with up-to-date occurrences that could make or break your business.

It's recommended that you post daily and engage on a daily basis so that you will maintain a presence in the minds of your audience. Just be sure you are not tweeting things that people are bound to overlook. Strive for useful, valuable, and relevant information that people want to click on and retweet.

Ask for some love

Don't be afraid to ask loyal fans to

retweet and mention your company in their tweets. Shared content is king.

Keep track of mentions and respond appropriately

As a business on Twitter, keeping track of brand mentions and keywords is vital to your internet existence. When you engage with others, always be polite and professional. Customer service is a big key to successful marketing. Twitter is one of the main platforms online where consumers post their questions and complaints. Monitor these conversations and jump in when appropriate.

Retweet

Retweet as much as you can without overdoing it. This allows you to link your business and cement your authority and leadership in your industry throughout the World Wide Web.

Favorite tweets

Many people overlook the 'favoriting tweets' option, but this can be a great way to grab the attention of other users and influencers.

Follow hashtags and trends

Keep up to date with trending topics. This is key when creating methods to stay relevant and connected to your brand in the future. When you place your business on the trending topics, your handle is bound to be seen, and people will then search tweets that are about your specific hashtags.

Always find unique ways to tag your posts with at least two relevant hashtags, just ensure you are not making your tweets look like spam, for they will be ignored.

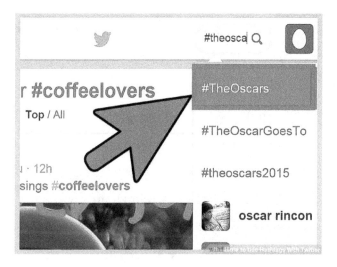

Offer special offers to your Twitter followers

Create Twitter content to keep people engaged and active with your company.

1. The next 75 people to retweet me will get a 50% off coupon
2. Post a photo of yourself in our store or using a product to be entered into our monthly drawing

Use videos and images

Visualization is a huge aspect of all social media platforms in 2018 and beyond. Photos and videos are known to drive four times the clicks on Twitter alone. They enrich your posts so that they receive more shares and clicks.

Utilize promoted tweets

Ensure you are using promoted tweets to your directed target audience. If you fail to do this, you will decrease the definition of who you are attempting to reach out to, which can cost you valuable time and money.

Keep promoted tweets fresh and ensure they don't run for too long. If you want to continue using them over a period of time, write posts with varying words.

Integrate Twitter with other marketing activities

Twitter, just like all other social media platforms, is best used and it's most effective when integrated into your other marketing activities. If you are running a promotion or contest on Twitter, for instance, email your subscribers about it too. By simply placing your tweets into emails, you can tap into Twitter through your email content. And that's just one other platform!

Learn Twitter analytics

Learn how to read the analytics of Twitter to get a good grasp on what kind of content resonates with your audience and what doesn't. You will be able to view what your best days were and the type of content your followers enjoyed and vice versa.

Chapter summary

1. Twitter is a great platform to keep your audience updated on current and upcoming company happenings through short, efficient tweets

2. Thousands of people are on Twitter, which means it's important to learn how to leverage the platform wisely for optimal use

3. Tweet consistently and use relevant hashtags, videos, and images to make your posts stand out

Quickstart action step

I urge you to create a Twitter account that is based on your business or industry and dive deeper into hashtags and keywords. Below are amazing examples of people and companies that have learned to leverage Twitter to their full advantage:

- Ravi Chahar (https://twitter.com/ravichahar27)
- Mediabistro (https://twitter.com/Mediabistro)
- Jorden Makelle (https://twitter.com/JordenMakelle)
- Jackie Sizemore (https://twitter.com/sizemorepov)

If you take a quick gander at these optimized Twitter profiles, you may find yourself in a deep rabbit hole of useful knowledge, seeing the people that follow these profiles and the profiles they follow as well!

Chapter 7:

Instagram

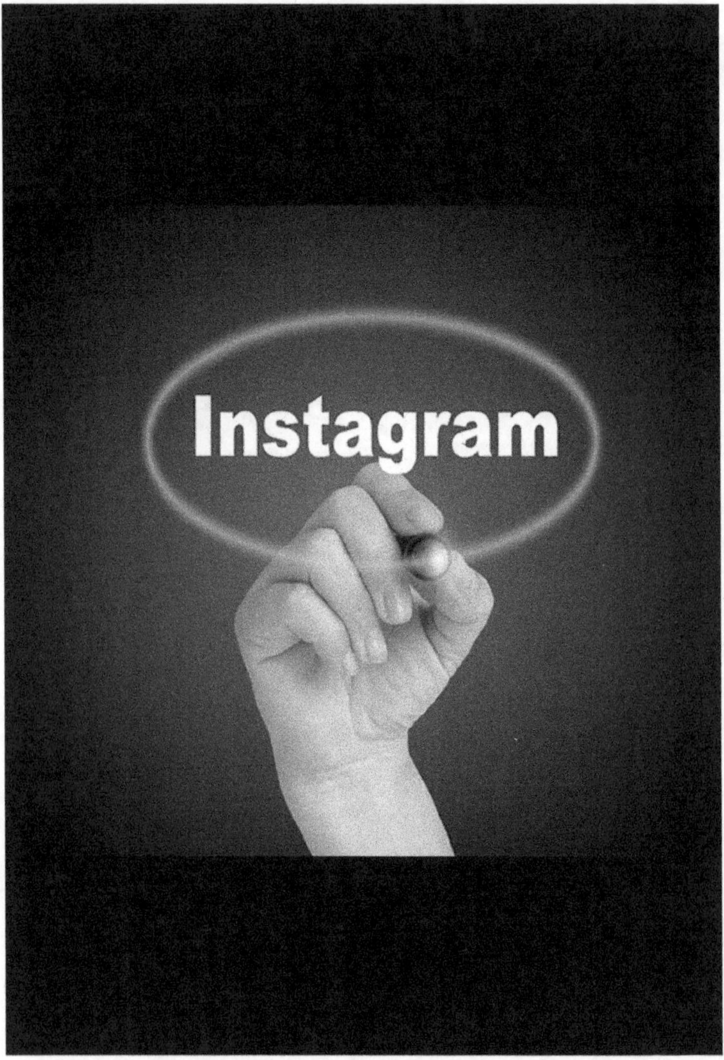
Instagram

Chapter 7: Instagram

Instagram is a social media platform that has been around for a few years, and it's quietly picking up amazing traction thanks to the trending obsession for mobile photography that doesn't seem to be fading anytime soon.

What is Instagram?

Instagram is a social networking application that was designed to share videos and photos from smartphones. Just like Twitter and Facebook, all users that sign up and create an Instagram account have a dedicated profile and a newsfeed.

How Instagram works

When a user adds a photo or video to the Instagram app, it's displayed on their profile. Other users who follow you will be able to see your posts on their feeds. It's essentially a simplified version of Facebook, with a deeper emphasis on visual mobile sharing. Just like all other popular social media sites, you can interact with other users by following, being followed, commenting, messaging, and tagging. You can save photos from Instagram onto your mobile devices as well.

Using Instagram

Before users can begin utilizing the Instagram application, they are prompted to create an account, free of charge. You can sign up easily with your email or with Facebook. You just have to create a username and password.

After signing up, you will be prompted with the choice to follow friends who are also on Instagram or on your Facebook network if you signed up via Facebook. Or, you can simply skip this process and come back later.

It's in your best interest, both for personal and business use, to optimize your profile by customizing it. Add your name, a profile photo, a quick bio, and a link to your website, blog, or other social pages if you have them. When other users begin to follow you back, they will view who you are and what you are all about!

Using Instagram to promote your brand

If you are looking for a better way to get your company, brand, products, and services seen by more internet users and grow a stronger following, then creating an Instagram account is a great idea and can be the solution you need to grow your business substantially!

With over 300 million Instagram users, many brands are finding unique methods to interact with this community to invest in maintaining their existing customers and gaining new ones.

The cool thing about Instagram is that a

majority of users are known to be shopaholics, with over 70% using Instagram to search for brands and companies. And more than 62% of users follow a brand simply because they like it!

Thanks to the internet, shoppers have turned to social media platforms for references and reviews before they hit that 'buy' button. The bottom line is that Instagram helps you convert shoppers into confident customers that continue to come back, which is what all business owners desire.

If you are an Instagram newbie, no worries. It's simple to get an account on this platform up and running with these steps:

Step 1: Set up your business Instagram account

You should have a separate Instagram account when it comes to advertising your business. The audience is the core of marketing success, so potential buyers don't want to see snapshots of your last vacation or selfies of you. You should rarely make an appearance on your business Instagram page. Here are ways to optimize your professional Instagram account to appeal to consumers:

- Include links to boost traffic
    - You only get one opportunity for this, which

includes a link in your bio at the top of your Instagram page

- Have a consistent name and profile photo
    - Ensure all pieces of your profile fit together seamlessly
    - Choose a name that is the same or related to your business
    - Keep your profile image consistent since the thumbnail will be seen by your posts (they should be professional and recognizable!)

- Write an interesting and informative bio that hooks viewers

- Ensure that the last thing people see is your catchy bio! You must convince them to follow you and your business

Step 2: Create popular posts that users want to follow

A picture can mean a thousand words, which is why you want to post photos that will drive your followers to continuously come back! Instagram has grown in popularity simply because it's centered around visualization. It's been proven on other social media interfaces that posts with photos and videos get twice as many comments and engagement than those with just links and text.

Harness the love for a visualized world by posting photos that can lead to sales:

- Avoid hard selling
    - Pictures allow users to see your products without you yelling and convincing them how awesome they are. Let the images do the work for you

- Promote with professional and creative photos
- Resize photos for professional quality
- Utilize Instagram's broad array of built-in editing tools to enhance images

- Create unique photos that are captivating and capture your brand's culture
- Offer promotions and announcements that are exclusive to followers
- Promote events and share insider access to followers

+. · annamcnaughty ⌄ .ıl ⚙

403 | 24.3K | 2,058
posts | followers | following

Contact   Edit Profile

Anna McNaught | Photography
Photographer
@thelikedphotocommunity | #thelikedphoto
anna@amcnaught.com
amcnaught.com | Photography & Design
Join The Liked Photo's Facebook group!
www.facebook.com/groups/thelikedphoto

Step 3: Get a larger following

Even if you are doing a good job at posting amazing eye-catching images, you will still need a strategy to convince people to see what you have to offer and follow you. Here are some techniques that anyone can implement:

- Use hashtags to help your discoverability
    - Use keywords and phrases that are brand relevant
    - Search popular hashtags that are trending
    - Collect a list of hashtags that have been big hits
    - Create your own unique hashtag
    - Use 5 hashtags to complement your posts

- Invite ambassadors and influencers on the platform to share your brand

Step 4: Boost engagement and create customer connections

Now that you have shared brilliant content and have a steadily growing following, in what ways can you further solidify your loyal consumers? The answer to that is engagement!

If you have a photo that has been shared by hundreds of followers, you are going to get tons of engagement. By closing the gap between buyers and sellers with adequate communication, you often receive feedback directly from past, existing, and new consumers. The following tips will help you build relationships to convert visitors into customers:

- Create inviting captions
- Use contests to jumpstart active engagement
- Respond efficiently to notifications, shout-outs, and messages
- Use Instagram shopping tools

Step 5: Measure your success to enable growth

Don't allow your Instagram account to stagnate. What you need to do here is to consistently work on attracting new consumers and visitors back to your profile. This means you need to take the time to learn how to analyze your success, research deeper into your target audiences, and repeat popular content:

- Track cooperation from fans
- Track the best times to post on Instagram
- Post consistently
- Utilize scheduling application to cut down on your IG time
- Pay close attention to the media that people like the most
- Direct your strategy towards goals that are realistic
- Use Instagram to create a community that engages with one another

Chapter summary

- Instagram is an ideal platform to use for more visual posts

- It's essential to learn methods to engage with followers
- Engage heavily with other influencers to view what they are doing and what you could be doing better

- Boost engagement with consistent posting and learning your audience

Quickstart action step

Schedule a time right now to set up your business Instagram account. Or, if you have yet to create your very own Instagram account for personal use, try that and play around with it! You will learn the most from hands-on experience and learn the ins and outs of this highly visual social media platform.

Looking for Instagram inspiration? Take a look at these Instagram profiles:

- Particular Paws
- Oh Boy Artifacts
- Never Ending Toys
- Small Cakes

Chapter 8: YouTube

Chapter 8: YouTube

The most popular video website on the internet today is YouTube. Founded in 2005, there are millions of videos that have been uploaded, ranging from funny fat videos, movie trailers, tutorials, and so much more. Anyone with internet access can share content on the YouTube interface, no matter if they are a large budget corporation or a teen with a cheap camcorder.

Owned by Google, YouTube is the second largest search engine in the world and is still the number one video sharing website on the World Wide Web, being available in every country and in over fifty languages, this platform is user-friendly for anyone who wants to post content.

Even for those that don't actively add content to YouTube, there are thousands of others that utilize YouTube as a way to see product and service reviews, DIY tutorials, lifestyle hacks, and more.

Tips for using YouTube to optimize your business

When social media is mentioned as a tool to increase business growth, many people immediately think of the two biggest platforms, YouTube and Facebook. Since it's a video sharing website, YouTube may not seem like a suitable tool for marketing, especially when it comes to small businesses. This is far from true, however.

Comments on YouTube are directly linked to Google+, which makes it one of the most influential platforms to date. Creating and sharing content on YouTube is a fantastic way to boost your company's overall visibility and adds credibility to your business as well.

When it comes to maximizing the

effectiveness of YouTube to grow your business, follow these simple tips:

Consistently post content

If you take a gander at the <u>most popular YouTube channels</u>, you will notice right off the bat the high volumes of content they update their profiles with. If you want this to be a marketing tool, you need to be dedicated to posting tons of valuable content on a regular basis.

There are many methods to produce content for all kinds of businesses:

- Webinars can be split up and posted as a series of videos
- Repurpose infographics into explainer videos

- Create tutorials that demonstrate your products and services

- Create short, easy to understand how-to videos showing viewers how to do something themselves

- Create a video showcasing your business's profile and history

- Interview people
  - Owners
  - Staff
  - Customers
  - Yourself

Use calls to action

You will likely have links to the descriptions of your videos. This is where you want to think about how you wish viewers to respond before you post. Ensure that you have 'calls to action' in the video itself:

- Ask people to subscribe to the channel
- Tell them how they can contact you for additional information
- Ask them to leave feedback and comments
- Ask people to share your videos on their social media accounts

Be interactive

As people keep watching your videos, they will begin to rate the quality of them and leave you comments. To ensure you continuously have momentum, you should take the time to monitor any feedback you receive in a timely manner. It's recommended to use a 'cookie cutter' response that is automated. Even if personalized responses are the best, automatic ones are better than none at all.

Customize your channel

Visitors who come across your videos will click on your account. Ensure that you stand out from the crowd! Personalize your channel with various links, images, colors, and other relevant information. This is a perfect opportunity for you to talk about your brand, show off your logo, your tone, and any related slogans that people may find catchy and want to share.

Really think about your video titles

People use YouTube in the same way they utilize Google: by using phrases and keywords that describe what they are searching for. Titles are meticulously weighed in the world of YouTube, especially when it comes to appearing in search results. You want to avoid boring titles and titles that are not descriptive.

Not many people are going to bother clicking 'Product Demo,' but most viewers will more likely click on something titled like: "*10 Ways to Save Money Every Day with (Your Name's) App.*"

Pick the correct tags and categories

When you go and upload videos to YouTube, you need to pick a category and enter keywords and tags. There are 15 total categories to add your video to, and there are tons of relevant tags.

Make sure that the tags you pick are based on what people are most likely to search for. You can manually add tags as well.

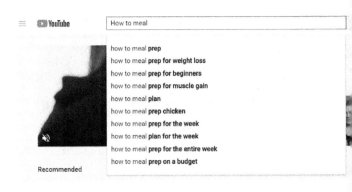

Craft an eye-catching description
The descriptions on each of your videos should serve multiple purposes. They

should be informative yet short, just one to two sentences that include keywords and a link to your blog or website.

Collaborate

Ideas that are collaborative are a popular occurrence on YouTube. Viewers really like them since it gives them the chance to see their favorite channels working together and adds great exposure for both parties. Pitch ideas to collaborate with other channels that will compliment your business.

Let your customers talk

Businesses receive further successful results via YouTube when viewers and consumers are allowed to create testimonials about that company's product and/or service. It's a very effective method to build trust with people and adds that extra push to get people to try out what you have to offer.

Utilize subtitles

You can easily use subtitles on YouTube via the 'auto-captioning' option. There are thousands of folks who have impaired hearing that really appreciate this extra touch on YouTube.

On the other hand, using annotations can annoy other viewers. Resist the urge to add pop-ups to your videos. Place links and your comments within the description area instead.

Build up your Google+ account

Social media is designed to be social, this means that when people comment on your videos, you should interact with them. The commenting system that YouTube uses is connected to Google+ profiles, so ensure that yours is ready for visitors to engage with. Include a professional photo and fill out all the fields regarding company details.

Don't be confined to YouTube

Even though you create and build out a YouTube channel, this doesn't urge people to look for you and your video content. A huge key to an effective strategy is to go out and spread the word about your channel.

When you post a new video, you want people to see it of course! Go out and share it via Twitter, Facebook, Instagram, etc. You can easily embed your videos onto your website as well.

Chapter summary

- YouTube is a great way to captivate your target audience with video content
    - Tutorials
    - DIY
    - Testimonials
    - Informational
    - Product/service reviews
    - Etc.

- YouTube is the second largest search engine on the entire internet; learn to leverage it properly, and you can see substantial positive changes in your business

- Take the time to engage with your viewers

Quickstart action step

Make time to go out and mess with YouTube:

- Even if you have yet to start a business or have no new products to review, take the time to make videos around things you already own.

- Adding value to viewers is key.

- Learn how to capitalize on using good keywords to get found.

Here is a list of both popular and up-and-coming YouTube channels so that you can have role models to model after as you build your own YouTube channel:

- Iampauljames
- Joshua Elder
- Freedom Influencer
- Tyler Pratt
- Zach Crawford
- SciShow
- TheOdd1sOut
- Income School
- Think Media

Chapter 9:
LinkedIn

LinkedIn is a social network built for professionals to use. If you want to explore future career options as a college graduate, are a business owner, or an executive at a large corporation, this popular social media platform is for people that are interested in taking their professional lives seriously and locating new opportunities to grow in their careers, as well as connect and communicate with other professionals.

LinkedIn is much like one of the traditional networking events for professionals, but it's done over the internet. You can add connections, communicate via private messaging, and jot out your professional experience to attract potential employers.

LinkedIn is a lot like Facebook in the features it offers. The features of this particular platform are just further specialized to fit the needs of professionals and entrepreneurs. If you can use Facebook, you will have no issues using LinkedIn.

How to use LinkedIn for marketing your business

LinkedIn has become such a great resource for business marketing over the years that it has doubled its membership in the last year alone. LinkedIn is a cut above the other social media platforms we have discussed when it comes to marketing your business.

To leverage the power of LinkedIn, follow these tips to optimize your profile:

Complete your profile

View your LinkedIn profile as your heart and soul, it's what you want to show clients and possible employers. It is not only a brand for your business but a brand for yourself as well. Having a rock-solid profile can give a rather good first impression of you. If you fail at this part, it can actually tarnish your reputation a bit. Here are some tips to keep in mind:

- Ensure that you add your real first and last name since this is the main thing Google will pick up

- Add your product and/or service

- Include work experience

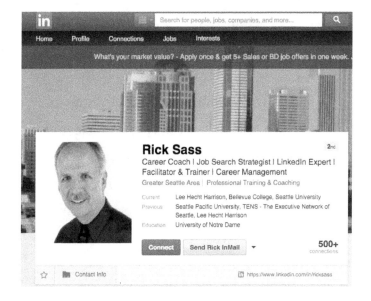

Rick Sass   2nd

Career Coach I Job Search Strategist I LinkedIn Expert I
Facilitator & Trainer I Career Management

Greater Seattle Area | Professional Training & Coaching

Current   Lee Hecht Harrison, Bellevue College, Seattle University
Previous   Seattle Pacific University, TENS - The Executive Network of
            Seattle, Lee Hecht Harrison
Education   University of Notre Dame

Connect   Send Rick InMail   ▼   **500+**
                                                     connections

☆   Contact Info   https://www.linkedin.com/in/ricksass

Connect

There are newbies to LinkedIn that
inform others to just connect with those
that you already know and trust. While
it's easy to understand where these
people are coming from, you need to go
out of your way to expand your
community so that you have ample

opportunities.

Instead of using LinkedIn to connect with folks you already know, use it as a way to network with strangers who may know just the employer or the company that can positively impact your career and business.

Customize websites

Creating a call to action provides more attention to viewers than just a generic profile link. Make it look sexy, and people will come crawling back for more of your beautiful business!

Be compelling

Many LinkedIn profiles are boring and have zero personality. Many view this platform as strictly business, which is an acceptable mindset, but to stand out among employers and potential consumers, you really need to have something that pops and catches the eyes of those that come across your company name:

- Add a video recommendation
- Tell people who you are, how you can help them, etc.

Recommend other users

Just like at networking events, you are there not only to ensure your own success but the success of other people. The more you give, the more you receive in return. Recommend others, and you will find that you will gain an increase of views to your own profile.

Get involved with targeted groups

LinkedIn groups are the bomb! It doesn't matter what business you are in, this is a big part of the platform you should focus your energy on. There are great benefits to joining and interacting with groups.

Connect with Twitter

You will find that <u>connecting your LinkedIn profile with Twitter</u> will aid in having more interaction and commentary from other users. Publish updates when you post on LinkedIn.

Add your company's profile

LinkedIn is one of the many platforms online that is constantly changing for the better. One of the things that are being improved is the company page. You are now allowed to add videos, share valuable information about your services and product, and provide users with more insights into what your business is all about.

Maximize search ranking

People search for other LinkedIn users daily because they are looking for the perfect candidate, freelancers to help them with content and projects, experts in their industry, etc.

This means you need to dedicate time to

optimize your profile so that you can be easily located and contacted by potential clients or employers.

Chapter summary:

- LinkedIn is a great platform to engage with other experts and professionals in your business's industry

- Taking the time to learn how to optimize your profile so that employers, clients, and consumers can find you is essential

Quickstart action step

I want you to go over to <u>LinkedIn</u> right now and start to create a profile! It's simple to do! If you are a business owner or entrepreneur, begin searching for other people in related industries as yourself. You will never know what amazing connections you will make until you try out this powerful platform.

Here are a few well-built LinkedIn profiles that you can look at for reference as you create yours:

- Shai Ortiz
- Mohamed Sikander
- Carol Tice
- Bill Kiefer

Chapter 10: Snapchat

Snapchat is another popular application among a large variety of mobile users. It is a platform that has drastically changed how people interact with one another compared to the majority of other social networks such as Facebook. Snapchat is mainly popular among the younger population of smartphone users.

Snapchat is both a social network and a messaging forum. It cannot be utilized for anything other than the mobile app on mobile devices. Users can 'chat' with their Snapchat friends by sending out photos and short videos. Think of it as texting but with more visual aspects. Users can also make video calls and text chats, two features that were added during the previous year.

Many other social networks give users no choice but to store their online information forever, but with Snapchat, once a 'snap' disappears, it's gone forever. This makes interacting online feel much more human, grounding users in the present moments.

Why Snapchat?

Snapchat is one of the quickest growing social networks, with over 100 million active users and 400 million snaps sent per day. Around 71% of the U.S. has an active Snapchat account with an age range of 18 to 34 years old. Snapchat is becoming a core piece of the global marketing strategy for thousands of companies. There are tons of brands that are utilizing Snapchat to create daily stories to engage with their audiences.

Ways to use Snapchat in your business marketing strategy

Here are the best ways that you can

begin utilizing this growing and ever-changing social networking application to delight your audience and grow brand awareness for your business:

Give access to live events

Snapchat is the ideal app to video events in real-time. This provides your audience with direct access to these events without them having to physically attend them. This is also great for launches of new products, shows, and other one-of-a-kind events. Snapchat has the power to excite your audience by providing them with an authentic view of your events.

Directly deliver private content

Snapchat is also great for providing your

audience with special content that they won't see or receive on other social media platforms. Use it as a cool little surprise for your Snapchat community of loyal followers!

Fashion brands utilize Snapchat as a way to show off their new collections before they hit the runway, for instance.

Offer promotions, contests, and other perks

I don't know anyone that doesn't love a good old social media promotion or giveaway; there are many ways that Snapchat has become the first choice for companies to use when it comes to offering promo codes and discounts to their fans that watch their Snapchat stories.

Allow fans a behind-the-scenes look

You can easily allow your loyal fans to take a peek behind the curtain to gain access to content in your community that others cannot see if they don't use this application. This gives people a unique perspective of your company. Capture company outings, parties, or just plain Jane afternoons. You have no limitations in showing fans how your brand can differentiate itself from the crowd.

Pair up with other Snapchat influencers

Just like on Instagram, you can collaborate with other Snapchat communities to spread awareness of your brand and expand your reach ten-fold. When you do this, you are changing up your overall demographic and expanding your target audience to a whole new group you may not have reached before. Influencers are skilled with the Snapchat platform and have the power to create awesome video content that can further promote your brand and gain attention.

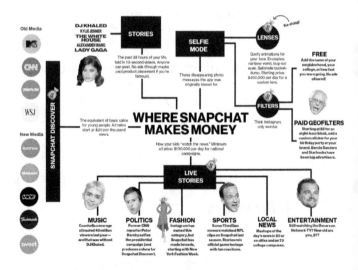

Chapter summary

- Snapchat is an amazing platform if you wish to make live events a part of your business marketing strategy

- There are numerous ways to make videos, and you can be as unique and creative as you wish

- Partnering with Snapchat influencers gives you the opportunity to leverage their following and expertise to expose your brand to a wider audience

Quickstart action step

I challenge you to create a Snapchat

account strictly for a business you are thinking about starting. Start to add people you already know, search for other people in your industry and engage with other users and influencers every day to begin expanding your overall audience.

Bonus Chapter: Using Facebook Ads to Grow Your Business

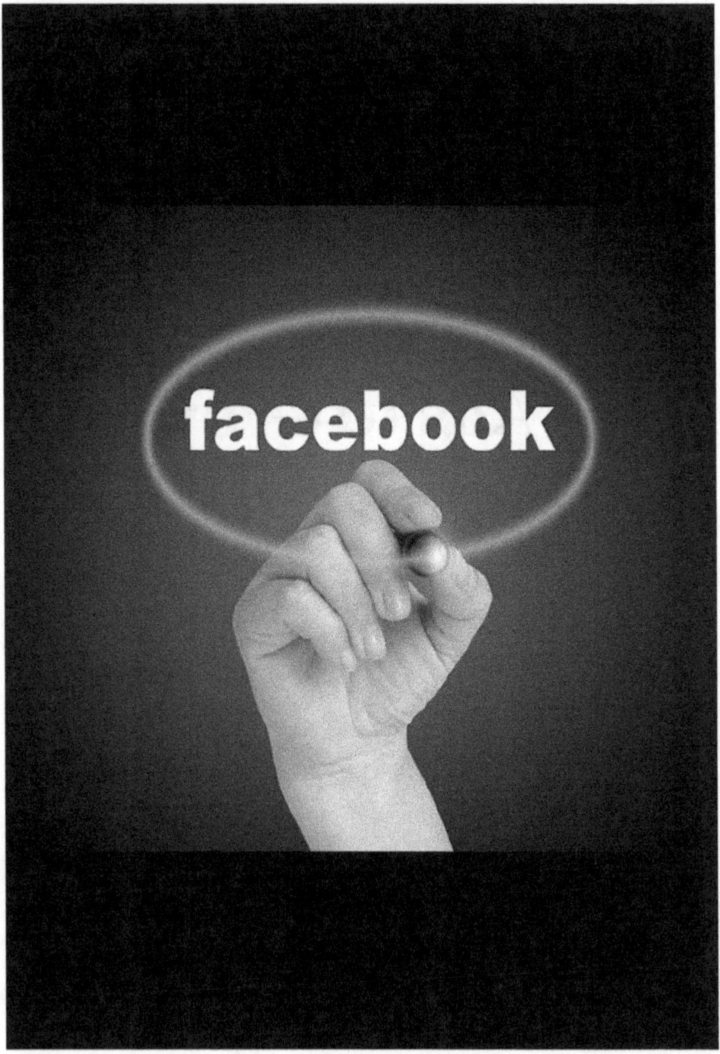
facebook

BONUS Chapter: Using Facebook Ads to Grow Your Business

If you have the desire to be prosperous via the Facebook network in 2018 and beyond, you need to have more than valuable and credible content. Marketing success in the Facebook world is just as much about distribution as it is about the content, especially as the organic reach from the newsfeed continues to decline.

So, how in the world does one get their awesome content in front of more people on Facebook? And not just about anyone, but to the right people in your targeted audience? The answer is ads.

The statistics of Facebook ads

Businesses in 2018 are turning to Facebook ads more often as a method to boost their overall performance in their content:

- 67 percent of businesses are planning to increase their budget for advertising
- 97 percent of businesses have invested in Facebook advertising
- In the U.S., it's predicted that companies will spend upwards of $120 billion by the year 2021 in Facebook ads.

Tips to get the most out of your Facebook advertisements

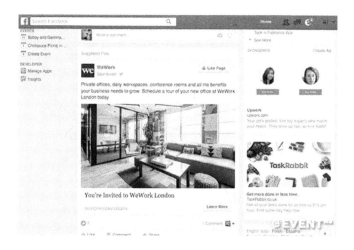

Think about who you are targeting

- What platforms do your fans use?
- What languages do they use to communicate?
- What kind of content do they engage with the most?
- Use the audience insight's page on Facebook to help you out.

Learn how to tell a great story

Storytelling is an essential key to communicating effectively with other people. No matter if it's in person, on social media, word of mouth, or written, stories play a huge role in connecting with other people.

If you are planning to put your ads on Facebook, remember your company's story and use it to capture the interest of existing and potential customers:

- Use creative and clear 'calls to action' to have people subscribe to you
- Use simple narratives that include an introduction to your brand
- Use articles about your brand

Keep track of how your ads are performing and adjust as needed

Obviously, social media has changed the entire world when it comes to the field of advertising. Back just 15 years ago, you had to flip on the television or listen to the radio to hear commercials and learn about new products, services, and upcoming events. People back then had no idea how to perceive an idea in real time.

Social media has enabled companies to monitor the performance of their ads from the very moment they make an ad campaign live. You can see your performance data via the Facebook Ads Manager. Here are some tips for a successful ad campaign:

- Clicks a bit lower than expected? Optimize call to action

- Engagement not where you want it to be? Create a new ad with creative updates

- Reach too low? Update the parameters of your target audience

- Make these edits to your current campaign(s), so you don't have to start completely from scratch:

    - Change ad creative
    - Switch up placements
    - Change your choice of delivery and how you optimize ads
    - Switch your schedule and budget

- ○ Change up your overall audience

Realize that your ads will not be perfect the very first time you go live. It takes experimentation and time to nail down the logistics to ads that deliver great results to your company.

Track your business's metrics

Before you go to launch an ad campaign on Facebook, you really need to get a clear idea of how you wish to measure the overall performance of your ads. This will ensure that you will kick off any negative aspects of your campaign and will allow you to assess the overall performance of the campaign so you can make the right adjustments and give your fans something they can consider valuable.

If you feel like your social media is not delivering to your fans as much as it should be, you need to experiment with the ads to see if paid marketing is not the way to go to advertise your business after all.

Think ahead in the long-term

The most important thing about Facebook is having a marketing strategy built for the long-term. This includes everyday social media interactions and actions.

For example, you create an ad with targeted engagement: Cool, but what is your long-term plan or goal? How will this first engagement continue to bring tangible connections to your business?

For instance, you are in charge of a fitness business that sells exercise programs online. You will probably create a video that showcases a simple workout in one of those plans. You likely aim that engagement at your target audience for them to view and get as many shares as you can.

You should be viewing this type of content as a starting point to finding brand new prospects into your ad funnel. You need to consider the lifetime value that customers are going to get out of your ads, products, and services. A rule of thumb is to aim your ads at customers in and out of your target audience. Learn to think outside the box.

It's your turn!

When it comes to growing your

business, advertising on Facebook will help immensely. I hope these quick tips will help you out!

Conclusion

Thank you again for purchasing this book!

As you have read, social media marketing is a prime skill that everyone who wants to make money online via these platforms needs to learn. Thankfully, social media is a marvel that will be around for many years to come, which gives you optimal time to work your way up to becoming an expert media marketer.

I hope this book was able to teach you things that you were unaware of and show you how you can begin implementing social media strategies starting today.

The next step is to take the valuable

information you read and start implementing it into your own social media accounts, building up other accounts for businesses, or building the foundation for a future online business you have in mind.

With the internet, anything is possible! You just have to be willing to learn ever-changing marketing methods and hone your skills to outrank the competition.

Thank you and good luck!